First World War
and Army of Occupation
War Diary
France, Belgium and Germany

39 DIVISION
Divisional Troops
Divisional Ammunition Column
1 March 1916 - 30 March 1919

WO95/2574/7

The Naval & Military Press Ltd
www.nmarchive.com
Published in association with The National Archives

Published by

The Naval & Military Press Ltd

Unit 10 Ridgewood Industrial Park,

Uckfield, East Sussex,

TN22 5QE England

Tel: +44 (0) 1825 749494

www.naval-military-press.com

www.nmarchive.com

This diary has been reprinted in facsimile from the original. Any imperfections are inevitably reproduced and the quality may fall short of modern type and cartographic standards.

© **Crown Copyright**
Images reproduced by permission of The National Archives, London, England, 2015.

Contents

Document type	Place/Title	Date From	Date To
Heading	WO95/2574 Nov 16-Nov 19 39 Div Div Ammunition Column		
Miscellaneous	39th Divl Ammn Column Mar 1916-Dec 1918 & Mar 1919		
Heading	39th Divisional Ammunition Column R.F.A. March 1916		
War Diary		01/03/1916	31/03/1916
Heading	39th Divisional Ammunition Column R.F.A. April 1916		
War Diary	Bourecq	17/04/1916	17/04/1916
Heading	39th Divisional Ammunition Column R.F.A. May 1916		
War Diary	Mt Bernenchon	20/05/1916	29/05/1916
Heading	39th Divisional Ammunition Column R.F.A. June 1916		
War Diary	Mondore Farm	11/06/1916	19/06/1916
War Diary	Zelobes	20/06/1916	20/06/1916
Heading	39th Divisional Ammunition Column R.F.A. July 1916		
War Diary	Zelobes	07/07/1916	30/07/1916
Heading	39th Divisional Ammunition Column R.F.A. August 1916		
War Diary	Bethune	11/08/1916	11/08/1916
War Diary	Bourecq	12/08/1916	12/08/1916
War Diary	St Michael	19/08/1916	21/08/1916
War Diary	Bout De Pres	22/08/1916	22/08/1916
War Diary	Orville	27/08/1916	27/08/1916
Heading	39th Divisional Ammunition Column R.F.A. September 1916		
War Diary	Orville	07/09/1916	07/09/1916
War Diary	Louvencourt	08/09/1916	08/09/1916
Heading	39th Divisional Ammunition Column R.F.A. October 1916		
War Diary	Louvencourt	04/10/1916	04/10/1916
War Diary	V 3a 5.6	23/10/1916	23/10/1916
Heading	39th Divisional Ammunition Column R.F.A. November 1916		
Heading	War Diary Of 39th Div Ammn Col.November 1916 Volume 9		
War Diary	H. 18. C. (Sheet 57d. 1/40,000)	12/11/1916	22/11/1916
War Diary	Valhuon	25/11/1916	27/11/1916
Heading	39th Divisional Ammunition Column R.F.A. December 1916		
War Diary	Noordpeene	12/12/1916	14/12/1916
War Diary	Ninnezelle	15/12/1916	15/12/1916
War Diary	Droogentak Farm	01/01/1917	01/01/1917
War Diary	Poperinghe	19/01/1917	19/04/1917
War Diary	Herzeele	21/04/1917	23/04/1917
War Diary	Court	29/04/1917	30/04/1917
War Diary	Hamhoek	04/07/1917	31/07/1917
War Diary	Near Nospl Farm.	05/08/1917	31/08/1917
War Diary	Heksken	01/09/1917	30/09/1917
War Diary	Kemmel Area	01/10/1917	15/10/1917
War Diary	Strazeele	26/10/1917	26/10/1917

Type	Location	Start	End
War Diary	Camp 50 Westoutre Area	29/10/1917	31/10/1917
War Diary	Hestoustre	07/11/1917	30/11/1917
War Diary	Poperinghe	01/12/1917	30/12/1917
War Diary	Ochtezeele	04/01/1918	04/01/1918
War Diary	Hamhoek	08/01/1918	28/01/1918
War Diary	Bray Area	03/02/1918	23/02/1918
War Diary	Nurlu	02/03/1918	02/03/1918
War Diary	Moislains	09/03/1918	11/03/1918
War Diary	St Radegonde	12/03/1918	12/03/1918
War Diary	Bussu	21/03/1918	21/03/1918
War Diary	St Radegonde	22/03/1918	22/03/1918
War Diary	Peronne	23/03/1918	23/03/1918
War Diary	Herbecourt	24/03/1918	24/03/1918
War Diary	Froissy	25/03/1918	26/03/1918
War Diary	Fouilloy	27/03/1918	27/03/1918
War Diary	Blangy-Tronville	28/03/1918	28/03/1918
War Diary	Boves	30/03/1918	30/03/1918
Heading	39th Divisional Ammunition Column R.F.A. April 1918		
War Diary	Boutillerie N of Cagny	06/04/1918	06/04/1918
War Diary	Boves	08/04/1918	14/04/1918
War Diary	Amiens	14/04/1918	14/04/1918
War Diary	Behencourt	15/04/1918	15/04/1918
War Diary	Saulty	16/04/1918	30/06/1918
Miscellaneous	39th Divisional Artillery.		
War Diary	St Leger	02/07/1918	02/07/1918
War Diary	Drooglandt	03/07/1918	03/07/1918
War Diary	St Janter Biezen	18/07/1918	04/08/1918
War Diary	Drooglandt	05/08/1918	05/08/1918
War Diary	Wardrecques	09/08/1918	23/08/1918
War Diary	Frevin Capelle	23/08/1918	24/08/1918
War Diary	Arras	27/08/1918	31/08/1918
War Diary	Wancourt	03/09/1918	03/09/1918
War Diary	Cherisy	04/09/1918	04/09/1918
War Diary	Hendecourt	06/09/1918	27/09/1918
War Diary	Sans Lez Marsouin	28/09/1918	10/10/1918
War Diary	Raillencourt	11/10/1918	11/10/1918
War Diary	Eswars	12/10/1918	13/10/1918
War Diary	Chateau D'Eswars	14/10/1918	20/10/1918
War Diary	Hordain	21/10/1918	28/10/1918
War Diary	Douchy	29/10/1918	03/11/1918
War Diary	Coutiches Area	07/11/1918	03/12/1918
War Diary	Hornaing	07/03/1919	30/03/1919

(8)

WO95/2574
Mar'16 – Mar'19
39 Div.
Div. Ammunition Column

39TH DIVISION

39TH DIVL AMMN COLUMN

MAR 1916 - DEC 1918
& MAR 1919

MISSING   JAN & FEB 1919

39th Divisional Artillery.

Disembarked HAVRE 8.3.16.

39th DIVISIONAL AMMUNITION COLUMN R.F.A.

MARCH 1916

Army Form C. 2118

WAR DIARY
or
INTELLIGENCE SUMMARY

39th DIVL. AMMN. COLUMN.
ORIGINAL.

(Erase heading not required.)

Instructions regarding War Diaries and Intelligence Summaries are contained in F.S. Regs., Part II. and the Staff Manual respectively. Title Pages will be prepared in manuscript.

Place	Date	Hour	Summary of Events and Information	Remarks and references to Appendices
	2/3/16		Column left Milford & departed in 8 Trains – 4 from Milford Station & 4 from Bodmining Goods – Entraining at Southampton the same day.	
	6/3/16		Arrived at HAVRE & detrained – the Column being under shelter of Point 6 until the following day.	
	9/3/16		Column left HAVRE in 5 trains and arrived at STEENBECQUE (Lillers) and THIENNES (Steam) on the evening of the 10 March, the remainder arriving on the 11th marched to NEUF BERQUIN – the last Train arriving on the 11th. The Column was attached to the 8th Division – and ammunition supplying	
	23/3/16		Lieut. G.O.C. Prater joined from BASE.	
	25/3/16		The Column moved from NEUF BERQUIN to BERGUETTE by march Route – the Divl Artillery concentrating in this area.	
	31/3/16		The Column moved from BERGUETTE to BOURECQ by march route.	

A.L. Syt
Lieut. Colonel, R.F.A.
Comdg. 39th Divisional Ammunition Column.

39th Divisional Artillery.

39th DIVISIONAL AMMUNITION COLUMN R.F.A.

APRIL 1916

WAR DIARY or INTELLIGENCE SUMMARY

39.DIV. AMMN. C__ Army Form C. 2118

Vol 2

ORIGINAL

Place	Date	Hour	Summary of Events and Information	Remarks and references to Appendices
BOURECQ	17/6	8am	Column moved from BOURECQ to MT. BERNENCHON (Behind Coubrires Plat (B.31.c.8.5) relieving the 38th D.A.C.	

A.B. Gotton
Lt. Col. R.F.A.
Comdg. 39 Divl Amn. Col.

39th Divisional Artillery.

39th DIVISIONAL AMMUNITION COLUMN R.F.A.

MAY 1916

Army Form C. 2118

39th DIV¹ AMM'N COL.

ORIGINAL

WAR DIARY
or
INTELLIGENCE SUMMARY
(Erase heading not required.)

Instructions regarding War Diaries and Intelligence Summaries are contained in F.S. Regs., Part II. and the Staff Manual respectively. Title Pages will be prepared in manuscript.

Place	Date	Hour	Summary of Events and Information	Remarks and references to Appendices
M'. BETRENCHON.	20/5/16	—	The re-organisation of the D.A.C. was carried out by absorbing from the Bde Ammn Columns. On the 20th the 3 Sections that are at midday from the B.A.C's such personnel and equipment as they required to complete estab. also all ammunition, leaving left their surplus G.S. wagons and all ammun at M. BERNENCHON. The 179 B.A.C. were taken over practically complete in personnel horses and formed the new No 4 Section, completing to establishment from the surplus left behind by sections remaining of B.A.C's. The Column is now billeted as follows:- No 1/5 No 3 Section X 1 a 4.2; No 2 Section N 29 E.8.5; No 3 Section N 22 d 8.6; No 4 Section N 2 a 19.	
	29/5/16		The remains of the surplus personnel, horses & equipment proceeded to Calais by march route.	

A.E.S. Griffin Lt Col R.F.A.
Cmg 39 D.A.C.

39th Divisional Artillery.

39th DIVISIONAL AMMUNITION COLUMN R.F.A.

JUNE 1916

Army Form C. 2118

WAR DIARY
or
INTELLIGENCE SUMMARY
(Erase heading not required.)

39th DIVL. AMMN. ORIGINAL

Vol 2 Feb

34 New A. Col

Instructions regarding War Diaries and Intelligence Summaries are contained in F.S. Regs., Part II. and the Staff Manual respectively. Title Pages will be prepared in manuscript.

Place	Date	Hour	Summary of Events and Information	Remarks and references to Appendices
MONDORE FARM.	11/16.	9 p.m	The D.A.C. received news that a large quantity of ammn was expected in the morning.	
	12th	8 a.m	Ammn commenced to arrive and was stored in barns at Mt. BERNENCHON (4 Sec) up to 1000 rounds per gun. 18 pr & 4.5. 8000 Stokes Trench mortar ammn also arrived. This was stored at MONDORE FARM. (Hadra SAC) The 800 Stokes were sent to the Dirt Road Store on the 17th the whole being cleared by 10 pm 18th inst. by the Div Lorries & wagons.	
	13		Ammn being delivered to Batteries.	
	16th 19th			
	19th		Column ordered to move ammn required units as follows:— Hqrs. R 27 C.O.4. No. 2 Section R 32 d 2.4. No. 3 Sec. N 24 C.6.0. No 4 Sec R 20 C.6.6. No 1 Section remained at X 1 a.5.2.	
ZELOSES.	20th		All ammn remaining at Mt BERNENCHON was cleared by 6 pm.	

A.E.S. Smith Lt. Col R.F.A.
Commdg 39 D.A.C.

1875 Wt. W593/826 1,000,000 4/15 J.B.C. & A. A.D.S.S./Forms/C. 2118.

39th Divisional Artillery.

39th DIVISIONAL AMMUNITION COLUMN R.F.A.

JULY 1916

July

Army Form C. 2118

39th. DIVL. AMMN. COLUMN.
ORIGINAL
Vol 4.

WAR DIARY
or
INTELLIGENCE SUMMARY
(Erase heading not required.)

Place	Date	Hour	Summary of Events and Information	Remarks and references to Appendices
ZELOBES.	7/8.		Column orders to move and occupied billets as follows :—	
			Hd.Qrs. 70 Rue de LILLERS. BETHUNE.	
			No 1 Sec. E.5.a.6.2. 6.8. ⎫	
			2 " W.26.a.21. ⎬ Bethune Combined Sheet.	
			4 " W.27.c.22. ⎭	
			No 3 remained at W.24.c.6.0.	
	15		No 2 Section moved to X.1.a.5.2. Waters to W.6.d.5.3.	
	24		Capt. W.F.H. ROWE from A.174 assumed Tempy Command of the Column vice Lt.Col. 220Cliff (Sick).	
	25		No 2 Section moved to W.26.a.21.	
	26		Hd.Qrs moved to 49 Rue de PONT NEUF. BETHUNE.	
	30		Capt W.F.H. ROWE assumed Command of No 2 Section, vice Capt. P.H. Porter.	
			& to remain in Tempy Command of the Column.	

W.F.H. Rowe Capt. R.F.A.
Commdg. 39th. D.A.C.

39th Divisional Artillery.

39th DIVISIONAL AMMUNITION COLUMN R. F. A.

AUGUST 1 9 1 6

WAR DIARY
~~or~~
INTELLIGENCE SUMMARY
(Erase heading not required.)

Army Form C. 2118

39th DIVL AMM N. COLUM N.
1 Sec 31. ORIGINAL VOL 5
August 1916.

Place	Date	Hour	Summary of Events and Information	Remarks and references to Appendices
BETHUNE	11/8/16	12 mn.	The Column marched via LILLERS & billeted in BOURECQ.	
BOURECQ.	19/8/16	7 a.m.	The Column marched to S⁺ MICHAEL via ECOUEDECQUES - BURBURE - PERNES - VALHUON - OSTREVILLE & camped in a field Ref Sheet 56 d. T.19 a 2.5.	
S⁺ MICHAEL	19/8/16	—	Colonel R.H. Carter CMG. joined from 37th Bde R.F.A. & assumed command of the Column	
—	—	21/8/16	The Column marched and bivouacked at BOUT-du-PRES marching via ST. POL - FREVENT. (Maps Ref LENS. N. 1/100000.)	
BOUT-du PRES.	26/8/16	—	The Column marched and billeted in ORVILLE - marching via HALLOY. (Maps Ref LENS. 1/100000).	
ORVILLE	27/8/16	10 a.m	All Small Arm vehicles & personnel consisting of 3 Officers 232 other ranks 58 vehicles & 301 horses under the command of Capt. W.G. Balen R.H. moved as a SAA Section to ACHEUX.	

H.C.R.
Colonel R.H.
Commdg 39 Divl Am. Colm

H.C.R.
Commdg 39 Divl Am Colm

39th Divisional Artillery.

39th DIVISIONAL AMMUNITION COLUMN R.F.A.

SEPTEMBER 1 9 1 6 ::

ORIGINAL
Army Form C. 2118

WAR DIARY or **INTELLIGENCE SUMMARY** 39th DIVL. AMMN. COL.

VOL. 7.   Vol 6

(Erase heading not required.)

Instructions regarding War Diaries and Intelligence Summaries are contained in F.S. Regs., Part II. and the Staff Manual respectively. Title Pages will be prepared in manuscript.

1st to 30th Sept. 1916.

Place	Date	Hour	Summary of Events and Information	Remarks and references to Appendices
ORVILLE	7/9/16	9.30 a.m.	The Column moved from Orville to LOUVENCOURT.	
LOUVEN COURT.	8/9/16	12 noon	The S.A.A. Section rejoined their own Section: a party of 1 Officer & men & other ranks, & 7 complete harness (P.S. wagons) being left to man bomb grenade r.c.	

A H Carter Lt Col RFA
Col Comdg. 39 D.A.C.

39th Divisional Artillery.

39th DIVISIONAL AMMUNITION COLUMN R.F.A.

OCTOBER 1 9 1 6

ORIGINAL

WAR DIARY or **INTELLIGENCE SUMMARY**

Army Form C. 2118

VOL. 8.

VOL 7

39th DIVL. AMM N. COL.

Period 1 - 31 October 1916

Place	Date	Hour	Summary of Events and Information	Remarks and references to Appendices
LOUVEN COURT V 3 d 5.6.	4/10/16	11 am	The D.A.C. moved via LEAVILLERS - VARENNES and bivouacced about V 3 d 5.6. (Sheet 57 d. 1/40,000)	
	23/10/16	10.30 am	The D.A.C. moved and bivouaced in fields at N.16.C. (Sheet 57 d 1/40,000). Before leaving at 1 pm V.3.5 Ammn wagons were handed to Corps without horses for use. All SAA Carts with horses were left at the Ammn Dumps for supply of Inf Ammn to the dumps for Artillery. Infantry still run by D.A.C. personnel. Large quantities of Artillery and Infantry ammn were carried during this period.	

H Carr
Lt Col R.H.
Commdg 39th Divl Ammn Column.

39th Divisional Artillery.

39th DIVISIONAL AMMUNITION COLUMN R.F.A.

NOVEMBER 1 9 1 6

Confidential

War Diary of

39th. Divl. Ammn. Col.

November 1916

Volume 9.

AQ

Army Form C. 2118

WAR DIARY
or
INTELLIGENCE SUMMARY
(Erase heading not required.)

39th DIV. AMMN. COL

VOL. 9   Period 1-30 November 1916

Instructions regarding War Diaries and Intelligence Summaries are contained in F.S. Regs., Part II. and the Staff Manual respectively. Title Pages will be prepared in manuscript.

Place	Date	Hour	Summary of Events and Information	Remarks and references to Appendices
H.18.C. (Sheet 57d.1/40,000)	12th/16	—	Nos 1, 2 & 3 Sections each detailed 1 officer + 44 other ranks - 120 trucks for pack animals. These parties were attached respectively to 116, 117 + 118 Infy Bdes, at BOUZINCOURT and MARTINSART, harnessing in Infy Transport lines	
	14th/16	12 noon	Above parties rejoined 39th D.A.C.	
	19th/16	—	All 18pr + 4.5 Amm Wagons on loan to Batteries were withdrawn to DAC	
	20th/16	—	DAC filled up with Gun Ammunition	
	21st/16	10 AM	The DAC moved billeted at:- HQ + Nos 1 & 3 Sections to LIGNY-SUR-CANCHE - No 4 Section VACQUERIE-LE-BOUCQ The Column marched via ORVILLE - AUTHIEULE - DOULLENS - HTE VISEE - BOUQUEMAISON - FREVENT. (at AUTHIEULE all gun ammunition was handed over to OT)	
	22nd/16	9.30 AM	The DAC continued to march via NUNCQ - HERLIN-LE-SEC - ST POL and billeted at VALHUON, resting at the latter place until 25th	
VALHUON	25th/16	9.15 AM	DAC continued to march as follows:- HQ + No 2 Sec via PERNES - AUMERVAL - NEDON - WESTREHEM billeting at AUCHY-AU-BOIS No 1 Sec via TANGRY - FIEFS - PERNES - AUMERVAL - NEDON - WESTREHEM billeting at WESTREHEM No 3 Sec via PERNES - AUMERVAL - NEDON - WESTREHEM - AUCHY-AU-BOIS billeting at RELY No 4 Sec via TANGRY - FIEFS - WESTREHEM billeting at LINGY-LEZ-AIRE	

Army Form C. 2118

WAR DIARY or INTELLIGENCE SUMMARY

(Erase heading not required.)

39th Divl Ammn Column
Period from 1 – 30 April 1916.

VOL 9 Contd

Place	Date	Hour	Summary of Events and Information	Remarks and references to Appendices
	26/4/16	—	The DAC continued to march as follows:—	
		10.20AM	HQ & No 2 Section via St HILAIRE – AIRE billeting at THIENNES	
		9.15AM	No 3 Sec via LINGHEM – LAMBRES – AIRE " "	
		10.15AM	No 1 Sec via St HILAIRE – AIRE " "	
		9.5am	No 4 Sec LINGHEM – LAMBRES – AIRE – BOESEGHEM billeting at STEENBECQUE	
	27/4/16	10.15 am	The DAC continued to march via HAZEBROUCK – WALLON CAPPEL – BAVINGHOVE – ZUYTPEENE billeting at NOORDPEENE, arriving at the latter place at 4.30 pm	

H.J. Carter
Lieut-Col A.C.A.C.
Col comdg 39th Div Ammn Column

39th Divisional Artillery.

39th DIVISIONAL AMMUNITION COLUMN R.F.A.

DECEMBER 1 9 1 6

ORIGINAL Army Form C. 2118

39th DIV. AMMN. COLUMN.

WAR DIARY
or
INTELLIGENCE SUMMARY

(Erase heading not required.)

1st to 31st December 1916.

VOLUMNE 10.

Vol 9

Place	Date	Hour	Summary of Events and Information	Remarks and references to Appendices
NOORDPEENE	12/12		The Column was inspected by the VIIIth Corps. Commander.	
"	12/12/16	9.30 am	The Column marched to WINNEZELLE — was inspected by the 2nd Army Commander — and billeted on farms around WINNEZELLE.	
WINNEZELLE	15/12/16	2am	The Column marched via WATOU and HIRSHOEK to DROOGENTAP FARM. and took over the billets of the 38th A.A.C.	

A. Carter,
2nd Lieut. R.F.A.
Commdg. 39th Divl Ammn Col.

Army Form C. 2118

WAR DIARY
or
INTELLIGENCE SUMMARY

(Erase heading not required.)

39⁺ DIVL AMMN COLUMN

1 – 31 JANUARY 1917.

VOLUME. Vol 10

Instructions regarding War Diaries and Intelligence Summaries are contained in F. S. Regs., Part II. and the Staff Manual respectively. Title Pages will be prepared in manuscript.

Place	Date	Hour	Summary of Events and Information	Remarks and references to Appendices
DROOGEN- TAK FARM.	1/1/17.	—	No 3 Section has remained the same. No 2 Section, & No 2 Section was spare up on reorganisation portions being out to Nos 1 & 2 Sections & the balance to 38th & 55th DACs, to complete AD Bce Am Cols. No 4 Sec 'B' Echelon became 3 Sec 'B' Echelon.	
Poperinghe	19/1/17.	9am.	The Column marched and took over billets of 55 DAC. Poperinghe. HQ, Rue des Pots. 1 Sec N7 & 2.5. 2 " G 4 a u.u. 3 " A 35 a 6 3.	
	25/1/17	5pm	The Column commenced to make up Battery dumps to 1000 rounds per gun, & completed by night DA4/30.	

A H Carter Lt Col.
O.C. Comdg. 39 DAC

Army Form C. 2118

WAR DIARY
or
INTELLIGENCE SUMMARY

39th DIV. AMMN. COLUMN.

1 - 28 FEBRUARY. 1917.

VOLUMNE 12.

Vol XI

Place	Date	Hour	Summary of Events and Information	Remarks and references to Appendices
POPERINGHE	16/2/17.	—	The D.A.C. came under orders of 55th Divl Artillery	
POPERINGHE	25/2/17.	noon.	The D.A.C. moved and relieved the 23rd D.A.C. taking over billets as follows:- H.Q. Place BERTHEN. POPERINGHE. 1 Sec G.19.b.9.P. West of " 2 Sec G.13.e.5.5. " 3 Sec. G.14.d.1.5. " Ammn Dump N.13 Central "	
			D.A.C. came under orders of 23rd Divl Artillery undel 10am. 1-3-17.	

H Carter
Lt. Col. RFA t
Colonel Comdg 39 DAC

WAR DIARY
or
INTELLIGENCE SUMMARY

Army Form C. 2118

39th DIV. AMMN. COLUMN

1 – 28 FEBRUARY. 1917.

VOLUME 12.

Vol XI

Place	Date	Hour	Summary of Events and Information	Remarks and references to Appendices
POPERINGHE	16/2/17	—	The D.A.C. came under orders of 55th Div. Artillery	
POPERINGHE	25/2/17	noon	The D.A.C. moved and relieved the 23rd D.A.C. taking over billets to follow:- H.Q. Place BERTHEN, POPERINGHE. 1 Sec. G.19.b.9.p. Shel 28 2 Sec. G.13.c.5.5. " 3 Sec. G.14.a.1.5. " Ammn Dump N.13 Central D.A.C. came under orders of 23rd Divl Artillery until 10am. 1-3-17.	

A. Carter Lt. Col. RFA
Colonel Comdg 39 D.A.C.

Army Form C. 2118

39th. DIVL. AMMN. COLUMN.

ORIGINAL.

1 – 31st MARCH 1917.

Vol/12

WAR DIARY or INTELLIGENCE SUMMARY

(Erase heading not required.)

VOLUME 13.

Instructions regarding War Diaries and Intelligence Summaries are contained in F. S. Regs., Part II. and the Staff Manual respectively. Title Pages will be prepared in manuscript.

Place	Date	Hour	Summary of Events and Information	Remarks and references to Appendices
POPERINGHE	1-3-17	10 am	The D.A.C. came under orders of 39th Div. Artillery - on departure of 23rd Div. Artillery.	
"	26.3.17	7 pm	D.A.C. supplied 1944 A.7.4.X & 792 B.X to gun positions	
"	27/7	"	" 2550 A.7.4.X & 840 B.X " "	
"	28/3	"	" 1140 A.7.4.X & 1260 B.X " "	
"	1-31	—	Work on the new dump at (Sheet 28) N.14.d.6.8 was continued during the month, & 8000 A.7.4.X & 1700 B.X placed in this dump in the 31st inst.	
"	1-31	—	An average of 20 G.S. wagons daily were supplied for conveying R.E. material beyond YPRES &c.	

H. Carter
Lt. Col. R.F.A.
Colonel Comdg 39 D.A.C.

Army Form C. 2118

WAR DIARY
or
INTELLIGENCE SUMMARY
(Erase heading not required.)

39 DIVL. AMMN. COLUMN.

1st – 31st APRIL 1917.

Vol 13

Place	Date	Hour	Summary of Events and Information	Remarks and references to Appendices
POPERINGHE	9.4.17	9 a.m.	B. Echelon D.A.C. were relieved at (Sheet 28) G.14.d.5.9 by B Echelon 23rd D.A.C. and proceeded to Reserve Area taking over billets at (Sheet 27.) D.8.c.8.6. They were temporarily attached to A Echelon 23 D.A.C.	
POPERINGHE	19.4.17	9 a.m.	H.2. and A Echelon D.A.C were relieved by H.2. and A Echelon 23rd D.A.C and withdrawn to Reserve Area taking over billets as follows:— H.2. D.10.a.t.2 Sheet 27. 1 Sec. C.12.b.8.2. " 2 Sec. B.2.c.5.7. "	
HERZEELE	21.4.17	2 a.m.	B Echelon D.A.C. relieved a section of 55th D.A.C. at Sheet 28. A.25.4.0.8	

A. Carter
Lt. Col. R.F.A. t
Colonel Comdg. 39th D.A.C.

ORIGINAL Army Form C. 2118

WAR DIARY or INTELLIGENCE SUMMARY

39th DIVL. AMMN. COLUMN.

1st – 31st MAY. 1917.

VOLUMNE 15.

Place	Date	Hour	Summary of Events and Information	Remarks and references to Appendices
HERZEELE	7th	12 noon	No 1 Section marched from HERZEELE to A 21 a 9.3. in relief of No 2 Section 38th D.A.C. & took up supply of ammn. to 174th Bde.	—
HERZEELE	15th	—	No Div. D.A.C. marched from HERZEELE to A 16 C 9.4. Sheet 28.	(a)
HERZEELE	23rd	—	No 2 Section marched from HERZEELE to A 16 C 9.0 Sheet 28, in relief of 298 Arty Bde Ammn Column & took up supply of ammn. to 186 Bde Arty Bde.	
Camp.	29	—	The D.A.C. handed over 74 horses & 18 mules to Batteries of the Divl Artillery.	

A.C. Ross
Lt. Col. R.F.A.
Colonel Comdg. 39 D.A.C.

1875 Wt. W593/826 1,000,000 4/15. J.B.C. & A. A.D.S.S./Forms/C. 2118.

WAR DIARY
INTELLIGENCE SUMMARY

Army Form C. 2118

39th DIV¹ AMM N COLUMN.
ORIGINAL
VOLUME 16.

JC 15

Place	Date	Hour	Summary of Events and Information	Remarks and references to Appendices
Camp	3rd	—	Owing to shelling No 1 Section moved from Camp A.21.a.8.3 (Sheet 28) to A.22.a.08 (Sheet 28)	
"	11th	—	DAC kept over VIII Corps Dump. A.28.a.8.4 (Sheet 28)	
"	18	—	Handed over Dump at A.28.a.84 to XVIII Corps. and formed a Dump at A.25 & 38.	
"	21st	—	Owing to shelling DAC HQrs moved to A.25 & 08 (Sheet 28) and No 2 Section to A.22.a.08 (Sheet 28)	
"	28	—	Owing to shelling No 1 & 2 Sections moved - No 1 Section to A.20 C.P.H. (Sheet 28) & No 2 Section to A.20 C.4.5.	
"	29	—	HQ Dump was moved to No 1 Section lines.	
"	30	—	Casualties during the month 1 Killed 1 Officer & 19 O.Ranks wounded, 19 Animals Killed & a number wounded.	
"	30th	—	Ammn conveyed to gun positions during the month	

32259 A74X 15.354 B.X.
32259 A74X 15.354 1,000,000 lbs of Wagon loads of Material were conveyed up the line during the month.

H¹ Cartero Col R.F.A.
O/Comdg 39 D.A.C.

ORIGINAL.

Army Form C. 2118

WAR DIARY
or
INTELLIGENCE SUMMARY

39th DIVL. AMMN. COLUMN.

(Erase heading not required.) 1 - 31st July 1917.

VOLUME 17. Vol 16

Place	Date	Hour	Summary of Events and Information	Remarks and references to Appendices
HAMADER	4/17	—	D.A.C. completed the filling of 6 - 18 pr gun positions of approx. 6000 rounds each & 1 4.5" position of 6100 rounds.	
	5/17	noon	The B.C. R.A. 39th Arty - Gen. C. Cullen D.S.O. presented Military Medals to the following men of the D.A.C. who were recently awarded Rbn. for gallantry.— Lawton to wit. 21751 Serjt B.r. Skipper, 47596 Corl. A.H. Holden, 118324 Dr L.A. Arnott, & 33470 Sgt L. Stamford.	
	7/17	7.30 am	HQ officers were flown up during enemy shelling of back areas	
	8/30/17		A number of working parties are formed during the month & ammn convoys by wagon & pack to forward areas.	
	30/17	9 am	A new Dump was formed at MS.O 55 Shd 28 for supply of 18 pr H.S. & Infantry ammn.	
	30/17	9.30	Casualties during the month - 20 officers wounded, (other) 2 men killed, 16 wounded.	
	31/17	9.	3 animals killed & wounded.	
		9.30 am	H.Q. & Nos 1 & 2 Sections moved & bivouaced in the vicinity of B.35 a 9.7 Shd 28 & commenced to supply Dumps.	M.Carter Lieut Col RHA A/Ding Coll 39th DAC Colonel Comdg 39 DAC

WAR DIARY or INTELLIGENCE SUMMARY

Army Form C. 2118

39th DIVL. AMM. COLUMN.

(Erase heading not required.) **1 – 31st AUGUST 1917.** ORIGINAL

VOLUME 18

Place	Date	Hour	Summary of Events and Information	Remarks and references to Appendices
Near HOSPL FARM.	5th	1 pm.	Enemy aircraft dropped bombs in the vicinity – 1 Bomb exploded in the 1 Sec. Lines killing 2 men and wounding 4.	17
	6th		H.Q. D.A.C. came under fire of H.E. & H.P. Shk.	
	7th		Whilst conveying ammn to forward dumps 1 man was killed, also 2 mules killed & wounded	
	8th		Whilst conveying ammn to forward dumps 1 man wounded	
	9th		50 pack mules were brought up from B. Echelon to assist in supply of ammn.	
	10th		2 trainloads of ammn were conveyed by DAC party to Admirals Road (C 22 central) (Ref 28 N/M) and dumped.	
	11th		1 Trainload of ammn was dumped at ADMIRALS Rd.	
	12th		1 man killed, 7 men wounded, 4 animals killed & 7 animals wounded conveying ammn to forward area	
	13th		6 G.S. wagons & teams were brought up from B Echelon to salvage ammn.	
	14th		2 men wounded, 1 animal killed & 3 wounded conveying ammn	
	18		1 man wounded 1 " 4 "	
	21		Salvage of ammn completed - about 3000 rounds were returned to R.O.C. dump VLAMERTINGHE	
	22 pm		D.A.C. of area relieved : H.Q. M.B.C.I.S. A Echelon M4 & 8 Jr. B Echelon Te 3 c 11 (Sheet 2P.) Convoy reserve mules by 39 DAC, & joining to 10 Corps D.A. Conv.	
	23		No 33851 Corpl 96 Hinsell, 33871 DR Frans & 38509 Dr. Rawlins all of No 2 Section were awarded the Military medal for gallantry gaining in carrying in wounded from Regt Dump & conveying ammn to battery positions by day & past during & battle periods 19/6 20/7.	
	31st		Large quantities of ammn & pack animals to bring up fresh ammn + water to magazine & Tract during battle periods 19/6 20/7.	

Att:(signature) Lt Col RFA Signed BN:

1875 Wt. W 593/826 1,000,000 4/15 J.B.C. & A. A/D.S.S./Forms/C. 2118.

Army Form C. 2118

JA/18

WAR DIARY
or
INTELLIGENCE SUMMARY
(Erase heading not required.)

Army Form C. 2118

Volume 19   1 – 30 Sept 1917

Place	Date	Hour	Summary of Events and Information	Remarks and references to Appendices
Hukskin.	1st		Relieved H.Q. D.A.C. at noon 1st Sept. D.A.C. took over BARDENBURG Dump. H.Q. & No 3 Section at HEKSKEN. – No 1 & 2 Sec. at M.3.c.6&9.	
	4th		No 1 Section moved to N.1.c.25. No 2 Section to M.6.a.1.9.	
	5th		No 2 Section moved to M.6.d. Cellars.	
	9th		H.Q. moved to N.7.a.8.5. (LA CLYTTE)	
	10th		No 3 Section moved to M.3.c. 8.0. (CLARENCE Camp)	
	12th		18 pdr position at I.28.c.5.0. filled by 13th (5000 Rds) BARDENBURG Dump handed over to 4th-1 Divn. 39th D.A. refilling	
			becoming HALLEBAST Dump. (N.2.f.8.7)	
	23rd		H.Q. & No 2 Y.S. Section moved to N.1.a.4.5.	
			H.Q. & No 1 Section moved to N.13.b.9.9.	
	30th		No 2. & 3 Sections moved to HON Camps M.11.a.2.1.	

Casualties:

L. R.G. LEWELYN. R.F.A. 41. Div. No 1. Section wounded.

Honours:

13410 Cpl. S. WILD. No 3 Sec. } awarded M.M.
66056 Dr. J. COOK. No 1. }

H.C. Clyfield Captain R.F.A.
Comdg. 39th Div Ammo Col

ORIGINAL Army Form C. 2118

WAR DIARY or INTELLIGENCE SUMMARY

(Erase heading not required.)

1 – 31 October 1917

VOLUME 20

Vol 19

Place	Date	Hour	Summary of Events and Information	Remarks and references to Appendices
KEMMEL AREA.	12 / 6 / 7th		H. R. A. formed a forward Group of Armies at x of 8. I 32 a 9.5. Sheet 28 N.W. 1/20000	
"		p.m.	HQ. Nos 1 & 3 Sections moved to the MERRIS AREA. & fulled – HQ in STRAZEELE, & 1 & 3 Sections in the vicinity. No 2 Section remained under orders of 87 R.G.A.	
"	15	11 a.	No 2 Section came under orders of 39 R.A. & moved to Merris Area & billets in the vicinity of STRAZEELE.	
STRAZEELE 26th			HQ. & Sections moved & encamped as follows – HQ. M 2 a 5.9. 1 & 2 Sec. M 3. C 11. (CONQUEROR CAMP.) No 3 Sec. M 1 d 7.3. (ARETHUSA CAMP.) Sheet 28. 1/20000.	
CAMP	29		HQ. R.A.G. left via HALLEBAST. & BARDENBURG DUMPS for 75th	
WESTOUTRE AREA	31st	"	No 1 & 3 Sections moved from CONQUEROR CAMP to M 2 a 6.2.	

A.H.Carter Lieut Col R.A. V
Colonel Comdg. 39 R. A.

Army Form C. 2118

WAR DIARY
or
INTELLIGENCE SUMMARY
(Erase heading not required.)

VOLUME 21.   1st - 30th Nov. 1917

Place	Date	Hour	Summary of Events and Information	Remarks and references to Appendices
M.S. TORONTO	7th	-	No 1 & 2 Sections moved from M.2.a.6.2. to about the farm at N.8.c.5.8.	
	19th 21st		Hauled HAULEBAST Dump over to 30th Div. Arty. 39th D.A.C. here relieved by 30th D.A.C. H.Q. 39th D.A.C. moves to POPERINGHE. No. 1. Section moves to G.4.a.31.h. 2 Section to G.10.b.1.8. No. 3 section to G.10.a.7.8. Took over "B" Ammn dump at I.5.a.4.9. (Sheet 28)	
	23rd		During the month D.A.C. salved approximately 8000 unserviceable found (18pr. Howitzer) 6000 Cart. 400 Change. 500 Fuzes from the area in I. 20. c. & d. and I. 26. a. also Index I.19., # I.20. & I 25. A gun pit started by No 3 Section for 33rd Div. Ba. Systematic Clearance of Fields from Amma in area WIELTJE. St. JULIEN. commenced.	
	30th			

[signature]
Lt. Col. R.F.A.

[signature]
Colonel Cmdg 39th Div Arty Col.
Colonel Cmdg 39th Div Arty Col.

WAR DIARY
INTELLIGENCE SUMMARY

Army Form C. 2118

39 D Am Sub Col

Vol. II.   1st = 31st Dec. 1917

Place	Date	Hour	Summary of Events and Information	Remarks and references to Appendices
Poperinghe	1st	-	H.Q. D.A.C. moved to hk. 6.2. at C.10.a.8.6. Amn. park taken over by R.A. VIII Corps. & continued to be run by No. 3 Section.	
		-	Talonge scheme continued. A new forage Talonge Park established at I.3.b. & R.E. Talonge Park. 39. DAC reorganized in 6 btys. in accordance with O.F. 6117 Ap. 4 & 8.17 (Part III a). Surplus personnel being disposed of to Div. A.C.; Vehicles & stores being sent to the Base.	
	22nd	-	39. DAC relieved 50 Amn. Dump at I.5.a.u.g. thrown w.s. Culoye park. Two post cars taken over, at hour 21.12.17.	
	25th	-	DAC moved to :- HQ. OCHTEZEELE. No. 1. Sec. to N.6.c.E.u. No. 39 Div N.u. & u.7. Sec. tc. to H.34.t.E.1. No. 39.5. Wagon Lines. to be used as II Corps Reserve park for equipment	
	30th	-	Precautions against Division - "Birles" - H.Q. 39 DAC.	

A.W. [signature]
Lt Col. R.F.A.
Lt. Col. Comdg. 39 D.A.C.

WAR DIARY or **INTELLIGENCE SUMMARY**

39 D Amm Col
1-31 January 1918.
Vol. 23.

Place	Date	Hour	Summary of Events and Information	Remarks
OCHTEZEELE	1st/4th		The Column was ordered to move to HAMHOEK AREA. 1st & 2nd Sections moved the night to STEENVOORDE to bivouac first, & 3rd Sections moved on the morning of the 5th, completing the AREA and marched on that date to new camps as follows:— move on the new camps as follows:— H.Q. A55d 26 (Sheet 28) 1st Sec. D 24 a v 6 (Sheet 27) SAA Sec. A 19 d. 19 (Sheet 28)	
HAMHOEK	8th		Buff and Amm Dumps (C05c26 (Sheet 28)) was taken over from 32nd DAC	WR
"	9th		1st & 2nd Sections moved to town as follows:— 1st Sec G 3 L 5.9 Sheet 28 2nd " A 07 d 92 " " SAA Sec. 32 DAC at N 4 a 4.3. Sheet 28.	
"	10th		SAA Sec. relieved SAA Sec. 32 DAC.	
"	18th		Div Comdr inspected DAC.	
"	22nd		Buff and Amm Dump handed over to 35 DAC.	
"	23rd		SAA Sec. new rehearse to A 19 f. 9. (28)	
"	27th		1st & 2nd Sections entrained at PROVEN try training with Bns. & SAA Sec in 2 portions & trained to MERICOURT L'ABBÉ the journey being 11 hours. On detraining Sections moved and billeted in following places. 1st & 2nd Sec. ETINEHEM SAA Sec CERISY	
	28th		FROISSY	

M.C.Whitefoord Capt RFA
Comdg 39 DAC.

39 Div. Cav. Regt.
Army Form C. 2118

WAR DIARY
or
INTELLIGENCE SUMMARY
(Erase heading not required.)

Army Form C. 2118

VOL 24   1 - 28 February 1918.   JW 23

Place	Date	Hour	Summary of Events and Information	Remarks and references to Appendices
BRAY AREA.	3rd	—	D.A.C. took over FINS A.R.P. (Visa thru 57C) from 9th D.A.C.	
	4th	9a-	The Column marched via CAPPY - HERBECOURT - BIACHES - PERONNE to NURLU in relief of the 9th D.A.C.	
	16th	—	Enemy aircraft active. One bomb on FINS A.R.P. killed 4 and wounded 5 men.	
	23rd	—	One man killed and one horse's saddling arms in Bray Area.	
		—	Over 800 wagons were supplied during the month for conveying ammn. material in the area. A coloursable quantity of ammn. was also — are a good deal forward more towards ampability Remove Standing? on Dumps Commenced by H.Q. H.A.	

W. G. Marshall
Colonel Comdg 39 D.A.C.

Vol. 25.

Reference AMIENS - Sheet 17 1/100,000

Place	Date	Hour	Summary of Events and Information	references to Appendices
MURLU	2nd		Nos 1. 2. &3rd Sections moved and camped just East of MOISLAINS.	
MOISLAINS	9th	8pm	Enemy aircraft bombed in trouble of camp - 1 man killed 1 wounded.	
"	11th	noon	Div H.Q. Canal via to GR.9AB.	
St RADEGONDE	19th	9am	All section moved to St RADEGONDE, & NB on PERONNE Rd for rest & training.	
BUSSU	21st	5.30pm	NB Nos 1 & 2 Section moved to BUSSU to commence supplying Base half area. Ea section Baas under orders of 39 R. Am.	
St RADEGONDE	22nd	6pm	NB 1 & 2 Section were ordered to move to St RADEGONDE.	
PERONNE	23rd	7.35am	NB Section 1 & 2 ordered to move to NEM - via CLERY. Orders to load to go to ROMPIERRE but eventually hurried on main road by may return HERBECOURT & CAPPY. and supplied ammn to Base.	
MERICOURT	24th	5am	Orders to withdraw via CAPPY to FROISSY - camps in FROISSY about 8am - supplies ammn.	
FROISSY	25th	9pm	Orders to withdraw to MERICOURT - SUR - SOMME . and arrived there about midnight	
"	26th	10.30	NB 1 & YD section ordered to move to CERISY. Move to CERISY cancelled and orders to withdraw to FOUILLOY started , arriving about 3-30pm. Ammn supply continued.	
FOUILLOY	27th	5pm	NB 1 & 2 Section ordered to move to BLANGY-TRONVILLE	
BLANGY-TRONVILLE	28th	10am	NB 1 & 2 Section ordered to move to BOVES. Ammn. supplies to Bar & dumps in French of VILLERS - BRETONNEUX. 1 man wounded by a shell while firing in the Camp.	
BOVES	30th	3pm	NB 1 & 2 Sec ordered to move to vicinity of CACHY - and arrive about 4pm - camping North of the village & supplying ammn to Bau in vicinity of VILLERS BRETONNEUX	

A.H.C... Capt
1.3.18

39th Divisional Artillery.

39th DIVISIONAL AMMUNITION COLUMN R.F.A.

APRIL 1918:

Army Form C. 2118

39 D Aus Cof
Vol 26

WAR DIARY
or
INTELLIGENCE SUMMARY
(Erase heading not required.)

1 – 30 APRIL 1918.

Vol 26

Instructions regarding War Diaries and Intelligence Summaries are contained in F. S. Regs., Part II. and the Staff Manual respectively. Title Pages will be prepared in manuscript.

Place	Date	Hour	Summary of Events and Information	Remarks and references to Appendices
BOUTILLERIE Nr CAGNY	6/4/18		All 18 pr & 4.5 Ammn Wagons of Nos 1 & 2 Sections were sent to an adv'ced Wagon Line & bivouaced about T.2.d.6.2.a 1/40,000.	
BOVES	8."	2pm	HQ DAC moved to BOVES. & an Ammn Dump formed at T.11 Central.	
"	9."	9am	No 1 Section moved to BOVES.	
"	12."		3 men killed and 6 men wounded while delivering ammn to guns. Ammn Dumps handed over to 61st Divl Artillery.	
AMIENS	14	9am	HQ DAC moved to M.19.a (South of Amiens).	
BEHENCOURT	14	10am	HQ 1 & 2 Sections moved to MONTIGNY AREA & bivouaced about BEHENCOURT.	
SAULTY	15	11am	HQ 1 & 2 Sections moved to SAULTY via PUCHEVILLERS & MARIEUX to refit & rest.	
" "	16	10.30	No 1 Section moved to R.28.a.30 in vity of 156 BAC and came under tactical control of HQ DAC.	
" "	30	10am	An average of about 2000 rounds of ammn a day to Batteries.	

9/5/3

AH Coates
Col RFA.
Comdg 39 DAC

14 39

39 Bat(alion) Army Form C. 2118

WAR DIARY
or
INTELLIGENCE SUMMARY
(Erase heading not required.)

VOL 27.   1 – 31 MAY 1918.

Vol 27

Place	Date	Hour	Summary of Events and Information	Remarks and references to Appendices
SAULTY	12	6 a.m.	No 2 Sec moved to D.15.a.v.c. (Sheet 57C) and came under the orders of 186 Bde.	
	18.		The San Section was disbanded horses mules being disposed of by HQ 39 Div and officers and men sent to 2nd Army Rd. Reinforcement Camp. F.11.D.v.E.S.	
	30.		As this unit is to lines of Comm'n 1 officer 1 man killed 1 man wounded 18 mules killed, 14 wounded.	
	31.		No 1 Sec moved to W.15.a.51. (Sheet 57C).	

H. Carter Capt. R.A.V.C
Comdg 39 D.V.C.

17

Army Form C. 2118

39 D Am Col
Vol. 28
1 - 30 JUNE 1918

WAR DIARY
or
INTELLIGENCE SUMMARY
(Erase heading not required.)

Place	Date	Hour	Summary of Events and Information	Remarks and references to Appendices
	8th	-	H.Q. D.A.C. moved to FOSSEUX and new billets in the Chateau & grounds	
	18th		No 1 Section moved from BERLES-AU-BOIS to HAUTEVILLE (SIC)	
	20th		All 18 pr & 4.5 ammn vehicles were cut down to 4 horse teams and the total reduced by 18 driving and 36 led per section. The surplus being sent to Base after meeting up the Div Artillery.	
	25th	9.30 a	No. 1 & 2 Sections moved to PAS.	
	26	9.30	No. 1 & 2 Section moved to St. LEGER (I 11 d, Ref 57a) and came under the orders of 57th Divl Arty.	
	28	noon	The Divl Comdr. Major Queens C.A. Blackfoot CMG, DSO, inspected No 1 Column.	
	30.	-	During the last 8 days there has been an epidemic of Influenza in No 1 Section. About 25% of the section being unfit for duty at one time.	

A.H.C.
Col. R 6th
Comdg 39 DAC

39TH DIVISIONAL ARTILLERY.

CASUALTIES DURING MONTH OF JUNE 1918.

OFFICERS.

D/174th Bde.R.F.A.	T/Lieut O.N.MASH, M.C.	Killed 1-6-18.
D/174th Bde.R.F.A.	2/Lt.A.J.APPLEGATE	Wounded 1-6-18.
C/174th Bde.R.F.A.	2/Lt.H.LUSCOMBE	Wounded 8-6-18.
B/186th Bde.R.F.A.	2/Lt.H.R.DAVIES	Wounded(gas) 2-6-18.
B/174th Bde.R.F.A.	2/Lt.A.F.TURNER	Wounded(gas) 17-6-18.
D/174th Bde.R.F.A.	2/Lt.E.BRINTON M.M.	Wounded at duty 1-6-18.

OTHER RANKS.

	Killed	Wounded	Wd.at duty	Gassed
174th Bde.RFA	—	6	3	1
186th Bde.RFA	—	3	3	40
TOTALS	—	9	6	41

39TH DIVISIONAL ARTILLERY.

HONOURS AND AWARDS - JUNE 1918.

KING'S BIRTHDAY HONOURS GAZETTE 1918.

D/174 Bde.RFA	Lieut.(a/Capt) V.S.BLAND	Military Cross.
H.Q.R.A.	Lieut.(a/Capt) T.MULLIGAN	Military Cross.
D/186 Bde.RFA	2/Lt. (a/Capt) J.A.W.GRIFFITH	Mentioned.
D/174 Bde.RFA	Lieut.(a/Major) W.JONES, M.C.	Mentioned.
C/186 Bde.RFA	Lieut.(a/Capt) E.F.CROWDY	Mentioned.
39th D. A. C.	Lieut.(a/Capt) J.E.SHEFFIELD	Mentioned.
A/174 Bde.RFA	Lieut W.J.MOSS	Mentioned.
H.Q.186 Bde.RFA	Lieut.(a/Capt) V.HILL	Mentioned.
39th D. A. C.	Lieut.O.C.ROSSITER	Mentioned.
D/174 Bde.RFA	25556 B.S.M. J.H.COTTON	M. S. M.
39th D. A. C.	57155 Sergt. A.McKENZIE	M. S. M.
A/174 Bde.RFA	L37347 Driver J.MACK	M. S. M.
X/39 T.M.B.	70205 Sergt. C.ROBERTSON	M. S. M.
C/186 Bde.RFA	L38423 Sergt. J.BIRD	D. C. M.
C/174 Bde.RFA	51066 B.S.M. W.HART	M. S. M.
C/186 Bde.RFA	77224 Sergt. W.M.ROBINSON	M. S. M.
R.E.attd.186 Bde.	312088 Cpl.(a/sgt) J.R.HEY	D. C. M.
H.Q.R.A.	202378 Sgt.Mjr.(WO 1) W.H.WESTON	Mentioned.
B/186 Bde.RFA	66562 Sergt. W.H.HEY	Mentioned.
39th D. A. C.	28305 Sergt. W.JOHNSON	Mentioned.

Army Form C. 2118.

Instructions regarding War Diaries and Intelligence Summaries are contained in F.S. Regs., Part II. and the Staff Manual respectively. Title Pages will be prepared in manuscript.

WAR DIARY
or
INTELLIGENCE SUMMARY

(Erase heading not required.)

Copy
39 D AA Bde
Vol. 29.
1 - 31 July 1918.

Place	Date	Hour	Summary of Events and Information	Remarks and references to Appendices
ST LEGER	2nd		25th DAB took over lines in relief of 103 & 3 Section under "D'DULLENS" and MONDICOURT and entrained for 2nd Army Area.	
DROCOURT	5th		No Section detrained at PROVEN & PROVEN & PROVEN and transfer to DROGLANDT Area. HQ & 5 & 6 to E27.C.38. No 2 Sec. E27.D.38. Hrs 57	
31 Jan 16				
BIEFVIK	18th	9am	No. 2 Section there under orders of 33rd A.A. and moved to F25 a 3.9 Hrs 57 FPK spot map 2 site for Reserve Weapon and Pon Shops W/27 FK	
			and W/34. 25 Hrs 57.	
			No 2 Section moved to F27 & F.5. Hrs 57	
	19th		FPK was connected to the night rests Low Pressure of the Gas Poperinghe System.	
	25th		1 NCO & 4 X & 3603 BX was thes up by HQ & 2 Section and attached to HQ Section and gun position.	

A. Carter
A/Lt Col RA
OC 1st AA Bde 39D AA

Army Form C. 2118

39 D Aus CCS
ORIGINAL
1 - 31 AUGUST 1918.
VOL. 30.

WAR DIARY or INTELLIGENCE SUMMARY

(Erase heading not required.)

Instructions regarding War Diaries and Intelligence Summaries are contained in F.S. Regs., Part II. and the Staff Manual respectively. Title Pages will be prepared in manuscript.

Place	Date	Hour	Summary of Events and Information	Remarks and references to Appendices
ST JAN. ter BIEZEN.	1st	9 a.m.	No 1 Sec returned to 2 Section at F.27.C.65. Sheet 27	
"	4th	9 a.m.	No 1 Sec. moved to E.27.C.33. Sheet 27.	
DROGLANDT	5th	9.30 p.m.	No. 1 & 2 Sec moved by march route via WINNEZEELE – CASSEL – BAVINCHOVE – PONT ASQUIN to WARDRECQUES & camped – No. A18 C14. 1&2 Sec. A23 a G9. Sheet 36 a. arriving about 6 a.m. 6th	
WARDRECQUES 9th	"	1	16 men were sent for rest in forward area under 59DSA	
"	10th	"	16 " " " " 31st DSA	
"	14th	8 pm	No. 1 Sec. moved to V.16 b 30 Sheet 27 & came under orders of 29th DSA	
"	15th	7 am	to D. " " " " recruits of HAZEBROUCK & crew under orders of 9th DSA	
"	21st	9 am	No 1 Sec moved to N.13.C.35 Sheet 27.	
"	22nd/23	..	No. 9 & 2 Sec. Detrained at ARQUES & No 1 Sec at ST OMER and detrained at AUBIGNY & SAVY respectively and camped at FREVING CADELLE.	
FREVIN CAPELLE	23rd	7 pm	16 ammun. Wagons new out to forward wagon lines at G.57.C. Sheet 51 F.	
"	24	"	Remainder of amm. wagons new out to forward wagon lines. WO DTS & OS wagons of 1st section moves to DAINVILLE. L.38 a.9.1. sheet 51 C. G. parks 9 officer & 30 OR new	
"	"	"	and to HORSESHOE DUMP DAINVILLE	
ARRAS	27th	"	No. 2 Sec. OS wagons moved to ARRAS.	
"	29th	9 am	No & Sec moved forward HQ at HANCOURT. 1 & 2 Section No.1 T. Au. O.T.K. Cavallini during the month 16 OR nominees 16 OR nominees 11 animals killed 13 animals wounded from 25.8 4-30 HQ Section 34 F.	

WAR DIARY or INTELLIGENCE SUMMARY

Army Form C. 2118

39 D Aus Coy
1 - 30 Septr 1918.
VOL. 31.

Place	Date	Hour	Summary of Events and Information	Remarks and references to Appendices
WANCOURT	3rd	10am	No 1 & 2 Section moved to CHERISY and bivouaced. HQ O 32 a 56. No 1 & 2 Sec. at U 3 L (Sheet 51 L)	
CHERISY	4th	11am	HQ 1 & 2 Section moved to HENDICOURT and bivouaced - HQ V12c0.3. No 1 Sec. U.11.c.9.9. - No 2 Sec. U.17.d.5.8. (Sheet 51 L).	
HENDICOURT 6			41 remounts arrived.	
"	18	8am	No 2 Section moved to vicinity of GOUVES and camped at K15 a 6.8. Sheet 51 C.	
"	23rd	.	1 Officer 34 O.R. with 60 mules for pack work reported at HENDICOURT. Balance of No 2 Section returned to H.Q & Sec. Sheet 51 L.	
"	23	.	No 2 Section reported at HENDICOURT & bivouaced.	
"	26th	1pm	No 2 Section moved and bivouaced in R valley about V16 c Sheet 51 E. 15 remounts joined.	
"	27	3pm	HQ 1 & 2 Section moved and bivouaced at W 27 c 3.9. 9 remounts.	
SAINS LEZ MAROEUIL	28	9.30	HQ 1 & 2 Section moved and bivouaced over to 174 Bde. and 20 animals.	
"	29	-	20 Animals & No 1 Section were handed over to C118 Bde. A large shipment of Ammunition was railed and handed in to Dumps between H.6 & 18. Abt 34 G.S Wagon loads of tanks supplies was collected	
"	30		and landed over to Bdes. Ld. Battery positions. About 15000 rds AMM. & 300 rds 2% were issued to Btts positions in addition a considerable quantity was packed from a forward A.R.P. & Btt positions & all available G.S wagons were utilised in supply to form forward A.R.P. Casualties 1 man killed 4 wounded 4 Animals killed 10 wounded	A.H. Carter, Lt.Col R.E. O.C. Coy 39 D AUS

Army Form C. 2118.

39 D Amm Col

1 – 31 October 1918

WAR DIARY
or
INTELLIGENCE SUMMARY.
(Erase heading not required.)

VOL 32

Place	Date	Hour	Summary of Events and Information	Remarks and references to Appendices
SANS LEZ MARQUIN	4/5		Bombs dropped on lines of Section I killing 6 + wounding 8 mules	
"	8		120 Remounts arrived + were distributed between Brigades + D.A.C. The latter was allotted 26 (13 to each section)	
"	10	11.30	H.Q. + Sections I + II marched to RAILLENCOURT arriving at 14.00 + took up positions H.Q. X 28 d 39, Section I X 28 d 85, Section II X 28 d 55 (Sheet 51f) 2/Lieut M.S. OXLEY & 2/Lt J.T. MUIRHEAD arrived from Base Depot 2/Lt G.S. GOODALL proceeded to Home Establishment Company Colonel A.H. CARTER CMG left for England on transfer H.E. SCHOLEFIELD.	
RAILLENCOURT	11		Command of the D.A.C. being taken over by Captain H.E. SCHOLEFIELD. Captain G.S. GOODALL adjutant went to A.O.D. 1st Army on probation with a view to transfer, duties of Adjutant being taken up by 2/Lieut W.E. MISKIN H.Q. + Sections returned to neighbourhood of ESWARS + took up positions as follows:- H.Q. T7 a 8.6, Section II T7 b 8.6. Owing to congestion of traffic the move was not completed until 21.30. Shortly after clearing the shell positions lines of Section I killing 1 + severely wounding 3 men. All wagons in tunnel out to supply ammunition.	
ESWARS	12	14.45	H.Q. + sections moved to T7 g F. 1.8 CHATEAU DESWARS (Sheet 51A) move completed	
	13	am	at 17.00. Colonel F.W. BOTELER D.S.O. arrived + resumed command. All wagons were turned out to supply Ammunition. (6.0.0)	
CHATEAU DESWARS	14	18.30	All wagons out on ammunition supply.	
	15	09.00	30 men turned out filling in shell holes, moving fallen trees &c + to made deviation	
		13.00	to Main Road Estts for Artillery	
		15.00	Officer + 1 NCO &10 men sent to A.R.P & T10 c	

WAR DIARY or INTELLIGENCE SUMMARY

Army Form C. 2118

VOL. 32   1-31st Oct. 1918.

Place	Date	Hour	Summary of Events and Information	Remarks and references to Appendices
CHATEAU D'ESWARS	16	17.30	12 Teams out on Ammunition.	
"	17	16.00	24 Teams out on Ammunition. Lt. D.B. Rickie resumed duties of A/Adjt.	
"	18	14.00	48 Teams out on Ammunition. 2/Lieut. M.S. Okell posted to 174 Bde. 2/Lieut. T. MUIRHEAD posted to 186 Bde. 2/Lieut. J.R. MONTGOMERY & 2/Lieut. J. HAITHWAITE joined from Base & posted to Nos 1 & 2 Sub Depot respectively.	
"	19	12.00	24 Teams Ammunition delivered to 174 Bde.	
"	20	15.00	24 Teams out on Ammunition. At 20.00 A.Q.39A. Bde. No 1 Section moved to HORDAIN followed later by No 2 Sect after teams delivered Ammunition and were located at N11.c.20, N11.b.35, & N17.a.25 (Sheet 51A) respectively.	
HORDAIN	21	03.30	48 Teams out on Ammunition. At 16.00 - 22 G.S. wagons conveying ammunition from rear gun positions to wagon Lines D.A.C. At 16.00 - 24 Teams delivered Ammunition to 186 Bde.	
"	22	06.30	48 Teams out delivering Ammunition. 08.00 - 12. G.S. wagons taking Ammunition from rear positions. At 3.00 - 24 Teams delivered Ammunition from rear positions.	
"	23	08.00	24 Teams delivering Ammunition to 174 Bde 1500 24 Teams with Ammunition to 186 Bde. 16.00 - 24 Teams with Ammunition to 174 Bde. 2/Lieut A. SINGLETON & 2/Lieut. J. FISHER joined from Base and posted to Nos 1 & 2 Sections respectively.	

WAR DIARY
or
INTELLIGENCE SUMMARY.
(Erase heading not required.)

Army Form C. 2118.

VOL. 32   1-31st Oct. 1918.

Place	Date	Hour	Summary of Events and Information	Remarks and references to Appendices
HORDAIN	24	21/00	115 Ammunition Wagons and 16 H.T. wagons delivering Ammunition to 186 Bde R.F.A.	
"	25		Came into corps Reserve (XVII Corps)	
"	26		Col. F.W. Barker, D.S.O. Resumed command. 39th Div. Artillery during absence on leave of Brig. Gen. W.G. Thompson, D.S.O.	
"	28	12.00	HQ 8th wagons attached from 209th Army Auxiliary Horse Coy supplying Ammunition to Brigade. At 14.30 4 HS Ammunition wagons of HQ 8th wagons attached at J23a25 shed 5½a. at 14.30-39.6 Bde moved to DOUCHY, and took up location as follows:—	
DOUCHY	29	09.00	A.Q. Z22d69. ½ M/Section No2. D16a83 sheet 51a. Lieut A.C.USHER reported 29/R Epsdaler 2/Lt A.E.C. VANDERSTEEN 2/Lt D.L. ROBERTSON 115 Ammunition wagons reported 24/12 and attached to No 5 Bde 222. ¼ moved to Douchy.	
"			40 D.S. 1 D.A.C.	
"	30	09.00	J.23a. 2/Lt A.C. WARBURTON & 2/Lt A.T.A. PRICE posted to Nos 1 & 3 Sections respectively. Ammunition wagons conveyed ammunition to 174 Bde 40 HT wagons conveying Ammunition from T23yd to T29d 13 Ammunition wagons conveying Ammunition to 176 Bde	

M.H.H.
Lt Col
Commg. 39th D.A.C.

WAR DIARY
or
INTELLIGENCE SUMMARY

Army Form C. 2118.

VOL. 33.   1st to 30th Nov. 1918

Place	Date	Hour	Summary of Events and Information	Remarks and references to Appendices
DOUCHY	1/11	0700	Came under orders of VIIIth Corps and moved to COUTICHES AREA. Arrived at 1600 hours and occupied following locations:- HQ.- R11.d.01, No.1 Sec.- R12.a., No.2 Sec.- R12.b.	
COUTICHES AREA	7/11		LIEUT. E.W. CLARKE & 2/LIEUT. D.G. JENKINS joined from Base and posted to No.1 & 2 Sections respectively.	
"	11/11		LIEUT. V. HILL transferred to Labour Corps Base.	
"	14/11		LIEUT. V. WARDEN M.C. joined from Base & posted to 174th Bde. R.F.A.	
"	15/11		2/Lieut. W. WINDOW & 2/Lieut. C. PHILIPS joined from Base and posted to Nos. 1 & 2 Sects. respectively.	
"	20/11		Lieut. E.S. WISH posted to 53rd. Divisional Artillery.	

J M Stephenson
Commdg 39th D.A.C.

WAR DIARY
or
INTELLIGENCE SUMMARY

Army Form C. 2118.

39 D Am Col
1st to 31st Dec 1918
Vol 34

Place	Date	Hour	Summary of Events and Information	Remarks and references to Appendices
COUTICHES AREA	3rd		Lieut. E.W. CLARKE posted to 186 Bde. R.F.A. with effect from 19.11.18.	
"			Lieut. J.E. SHEFFIELD posted to 144 Bde. R.F.A.	
"			Lieut. J.E. WARNER, M.C. from 186 Bde. to command No. 2 Sect.	
			Work except work near river during however got teams out to	
			Sections for ploughing — wagons employed in carting certains	
			during the winter months or	
			of large cheese had bites for the remainder of the men	
			of 39 D.A.C.	
			17 Men in Hosp Leave during Dec.mbr	

Ashenfield Col
Cmdg
39 D.A.C.

Army Form C. 2118.

39 Dw Cul
Vol 36

WAR DIARY
or
INTELLIGENCE SUMMARY.
(Erase heading not required.)

Place	Date	Hour	Summary of Events and Information	Remarks and references to Appendices
HORNAING	7/3/19		Lieut H.C WARBURTON appointed a/Captain and Adjutant.	
	11/3/19		Lieut MR PITMAN posted to 49th Divl Artillery } Volunteers for Army of Occupation.	
	"		Lieut OC ROSSITER " " "	
	"		Lieut W WINDOW " " "	
			48 ORs (Retainable personnel & Volunteers for Army of Occupation) posted to HQ Divisional Artillery	
	15/3/19		Capt A BROWN RAMC to UK for demobilization.	
	17/3/19		ODG moved from COSTICHE'S Area to HORNAING.	
	20/3/19		Capt H C SCHOFIELD admitted to Field Ambulance. The column is cut down to establ. A. only 4 horses, 6 officers 145 ORs remaining —	
			Casualties during month 1 Officer 4 ORs	

M M Sutton
Colonel RA
Comdg 39 DA

www.ingramcontent.com/pod-product-compliance
Lightning Source LLC
Chambersburg PA
CBHW081244170426
43191CB00034B/2033